SCHOLASTIC

26 Read & Write Mini-Books

Beginning Sounds From A to Z

BY NANCY I. SANDERS

DEDICATION

I dedicate this book to my wonderful in-laws, Larry and Virginia Sanders.
Knowing you and being a part of your family has given me the happiest years of my life.
May God continue to bless you and keep you always!

Cover design by Maria Lilja
Cover and interior artwork by Anne Kennedy
Interior design by Sydney Wright

ISBN: 0-439-57627-X
Copyright © 2006 by Nancy I. Sanders
All rights reserved.
Printed in the U.S.A.

3 4 5 6 7 8 9 10   40   14 13 12 11 10 09 08 07

NEW YORK • TORONTO • LONDON • AUCKLAND • SYDNEY
MEXICO CITY • NEW DELHI • HONG KONG • BUENOS AIRES

Teaching *Resources*

Contents

About This Book 3

Alphabet Stories A–Z

About This Book

The letters of the alphabet are the building blocks of our language. In order for young children to acquire a firm command of language skills, they must first learn to master with ease the mystery of the alphabet and the sounds that different letters make. The appealing, alliterative mini-books in this collection will spark the interest and enthusiam of your students to help them build automaticity and fluency, expand their vocabulary, improve comprehension, and sharpen writing and spelling skills. The stories will help children begin to move with familiarity and ease in the world of language, and help them develop a lifelong love of reading!

Making the Mini-Books

Follow these steps to copy and put together the mini-books.

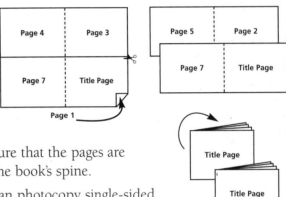

✴ Remove the mini-book pages along the perforated lines. Make a double-sided copy on 8 ½- by 11-inch paper.

✴ Cut the page in half along the solid line.

✴ Place page 2 behind the title page.

✴ Fold the pages in half along the dotted line. Check to be sure that the pages are in the proper order, and then staple them together along the book's spine.

NOTE: If you do not wish to make double-sided copies, you can photocopy single-sided copies of each page, cut apart the mini-book pages, and stack them together in order, with the title page on top. Staple the pages together along the left-hand side.

Inside the Mini-Books

Each book tells a humorous one-sentence story that incorporates four key words beginning with the same letter of the alphabet. For example, in the mini-book for *Aa*, the words *alligator*, *apple*, *ape*, and *act* all begin with the letter *Aa* and represent both the short and long vowel sounds of this letter. The books all follow the same format and include clear illustrations to aid in comprehension.

✴ The cover introduces children to the first key word that begins with the featured letter—*Alligator*, representing the short-*a* sound. Children can practice writing the letter by tracing the dotted lines, in this case, capital *A*.

✴ Pages 1 and 2 introduce the second key word in the sentence, *ape*, an example of a word beginning with the long-*a* sound. Again children trace the letter.

✴ Pages 3 and 4 extend the story, introducing and reinforcing a third key word, *apples*.

✴ Pages 5 and 6 introduce and reinforce the fourth key word, *ants*, and complete the story.

✴ On the back cover, children revisit the four featured words. They write the missing letter on each blank line and trace the remaining letters of each word.

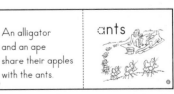

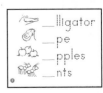

Teaching Tips

✳ Begin by first reading aloud the mini-books to children so that they can listen to the alliteration and rhythm of the words in the stories. Then encourage children to read aloud each story in unison, with partners, or individually. Repeated practice will help them build automaticity and fluency and gain confidence in reading.

✳ Let children use colored markers to trace the letters in their mini-books to help their writing show up better.

NOTE: The mini-books in this collection focus on common beginning sounds for the letters of the alphabet. However, certain letters actually have a variety of sounds. For example, in addition to its short and long vowel sound, the letter *a* at the beginning of a word might have a schwa sound (*ə*), as in *again, above, alone,* and *afraid*; or an *r*-controlled sound (*ä*), as in *arch, arm,* and *art.*

MEETING THE
LANGUAGE ARTS
STANDARDS

The mini-books and activities in this book are designed to support you in meeting the following early childhood standards as outlined by Mid-continent Research for Education and Learning (McRel), an organization that collects and synthesizes national and state K–12 standards.

Uses the general skills and strategies of the reading process and grammatical and mechanical conventions in writing:

▲ Uses meaning clues (title, cover, story topic, illustrations) to aid comprehension

▲ Uses phonetic analysis (common letter-sound relationships, beginning consonants, vowel sounds) to decode unknown words

▲ Understands level-appropriate sight words and vocabulary

▲ Uses structural analysis (syllables, spelling patterns) to decode unknown words

▲ Uses conventions of print (forms letters in print, writes from left to right)

Source: *Content Knowledge: A Compendium of Standards and Benchmarks for K–12 Education* (4th ed.). Mid-continent Research for Education and Learning, 2004.

Activities to Extend Learning

Word Cards

Make multiple copies of the word cards on pages 6–12 and cut them apart. These are the 104 words featured in the mini-books. (Or use the blank cards on page 12 to make your own word cards featuring high-frequency words or other vocabulary words you would like students to focus on.) Suggestions for using the word cards follow.

Alphabet Sound Soup

Stir up an imaginary pot of soup that contains words that all start with the same letter of the alphabet!

Bring in a big cooking pot. On a sheet of paper, write the letter you are focusing on and tape it to the pot. Next to the pot, set a basket containing pencils and construction paper vegetables, such as orange-triangle carrots, green-rectangle beans, and yellow-oval corncobs. Glue each of the four word cards that feature the focus letter to a paper vegetable and put them in the pot. Throughout the week, invite children to write on the vegetables other words that begin with that alphabet letter and add them to the pot. At the end of the week, serve up the imaginary alphabet soup by reviewing with children all the words in the pot.

Alphabet Train Word Wall

Make a word-wall train that contains a boxcar for each letter of the alphabet.

Mount a paper train engine on the wall. (Draw and cut out a simple construction paper engine or photocopy a picture, enlarge it, and cut it out.) Use 26 rectangular sheets of paper for the boxcars, labeling each with a letter of the alphabet from A to Z. On the first boxcar, attach the four word cards that begin with the letter *Aa* and review the words with children. Repeat for each new letter of the alphabet until you have a long word-wall train, featuring all the word cards from the mini-books. Provide blank word cards for children to add other words they encounter and attach them to the appropriate boxcar on the train.

Planting Words

Help children grow into great readers with this fun activity.

Give each student a paper cup filled halfway with dried brown beans. Provide craft sticks, scissors, glue, and colorful construction paper. Then give each child a set of word cards from one of the mini-books. Invite children to cut out four flower shapes from the paper, glue one word card to each flower, and glue each flower to a craft stick. Then have them practice reading the words on their flowers. As they read each word, have them "plant" their flowers in their cup. Send the flower pots home for extra practice.

 alligator

 ape

 apples

 ants

 boy

 bark

 barn

 basket

 cow

 city

 candy

 calf

 donkey

 deer

 drive

 dance

 Ed

 elephant

 eagle

 eggs

 fox

 father

 fiddles

 fish

 giant

 goat

 grass

 gum

 Hannah

 horse

 hill

 help

 inchworm

 itch

 ivy

 island

 judge

 jet

 jars

 jam

 Ken

 kitten

 key

 king

 lizard

 ladder

leap

 laps

26 Read & Write Mini-Books: Beginning Sounds From A to Z Scholastic Teaching Resources

 man

 movie

 monster

 moon

 Nate

 net

 north

 nest

 ostrich

 over

 otter

 ocean

 penguin

 path

 party

 pool

 quail

 quarter

 quilt

 queen

 rat

 roof

 ride

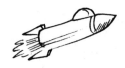 rocket

 seal

 sea

 sack

 soap

 Tina

 ticket

 tigers

 toes

26 Read & Write Mini-Books: Beginning Sounds From A to Z Scholastic Teaching Resources

 uncle

 umbrella

 up

 unicorn

 Vic

 van

 village

 vegetables

 Wendy

 well

 water

 whale

 ox

 box

 fox

 chicken pox

 Yan

 yak

 yard

 yarn

 Zack

 zipper

 zip

 zebra

26 Read & Write Mini-Books: Beginning Sounds From A to Z Scholastic Teaching Resources

❸

An alligator
and an ape
share their apples ...

An Alligator

26 Read & Write Mini-Books: Beginning Sounds From A to Z   Scholastic Teaching Resources

apples

❹

lligator

pe

pples

nts

❼

2

ape

1

An alligator
and an ape . . .

5

An alligator
and an ape
share their apples
with the ants.

6

ants

The boy
heard a bark
in the barn . . .

The Boy

barn

__oy

__ark

__arn

__asket

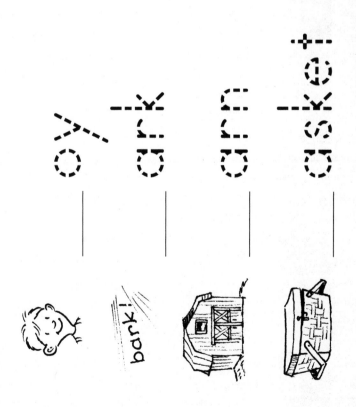

The boy
heard a bark . . .

1

bark

bark!

2

basket

6

The boy
heard a bark
in the barn
from a basket.

5

A cow
in the city
got some candy . . .

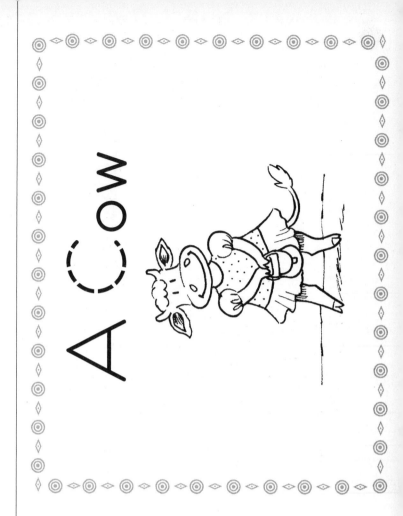

26 Read & Write Mini-Books: Beginning Sounds From A to Z   Scholastic Teaching Resources

candy

candy

city

mow

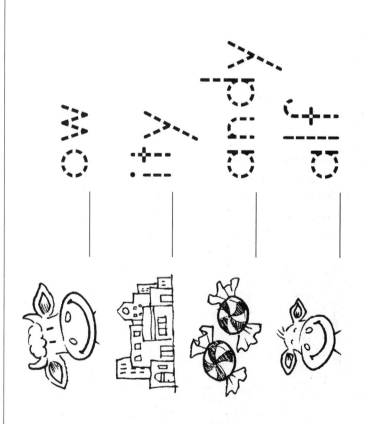

1

A cow
in the city…

2

city

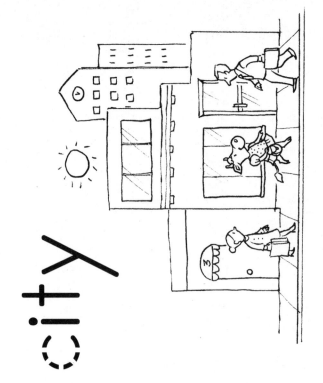

6

calf

5

A cow
in the city
got some candy
for her calf.

3

The donkey
and the deer
like to drive . . .

The Donkey

26 Read & Write Mini-Books: Beginning Sounds From A to Z Scholastic Teaching Resources

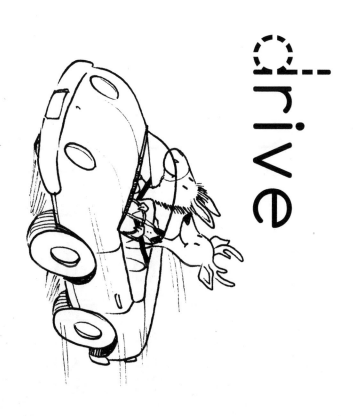

drive

4

__onkey

__eer

__rive

__uck

7

The donkey
and the deer . . .

deer

dance

The donkey
and the deer
like to drive
to the dance.

3

Ed
rode an elephant
to find an eagle . . .

Ed

4

eagle

7

E d

e l e p h a n t

e a g l e

e g g s

Ed
rode an elephant . . .

elephant

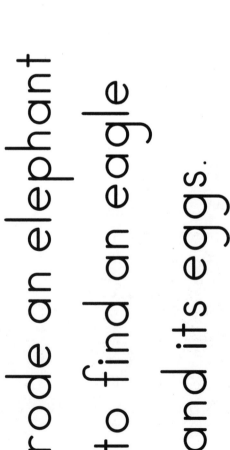

eggs

Ed
rode an elephant
to find an eagle
and its eggs.

The Fox

The fox
and his father
play their fiddles . . .

fiddles

ox

ather

iddles

ish

1

The fox
and his father . . .

2

father

6

fish

5

The fox
and his father
play their fiddles
for the fish.

A giant
has a goat
that eats grass . . .

A Giant

26 Read & Write Mini-Books: Beginning Sounds From A to Z   Scholastic Teaching Resources

grass

_iant _____

_oat _____

_rass _____

_um _____

1

A giant
has a goat ...

2

goat

5

A giant
has a goat
that eats grass
and chews gum.

6

gum

Hannah
rode her horse
up a hill . . .

Hannah

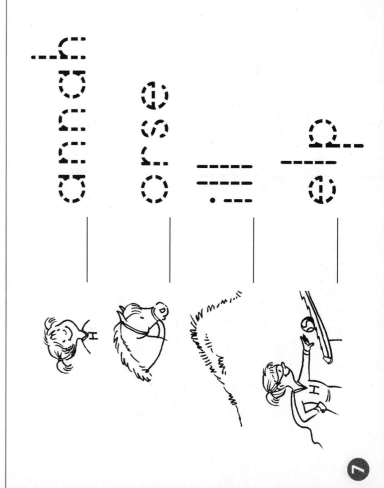

hill

annah

orse

hill

ide

1

Hannah
rode her horse . . .

2

horse

6

help

5

Hannah
rode her horse
up a hill
to help.

The inchworm
got an itch
from the ivy ...

The inchworm

26 Read & Write Mini-Books: Beginning Sounds From A to Z   Scholastic Teaching Resources

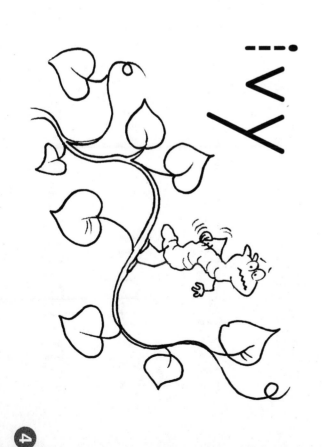

ivy

nchworm

tch

vy

sland

The inchworm
got an itch . . .

itch

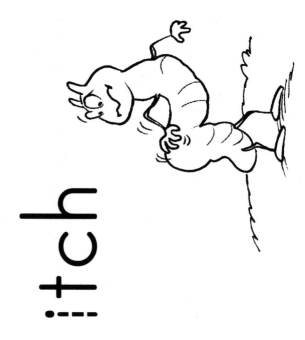

island

The inchworm
got an itch
from the ivy
on the island.

The judge
took a jet
to buy jars . . .

The Judge

26 Read & Write Mini-Books: Beginning Sounds From A to Z   Scholastic Teaching Resources

jars

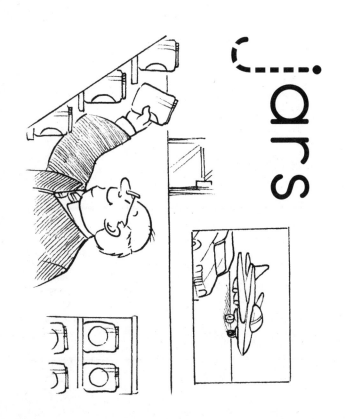

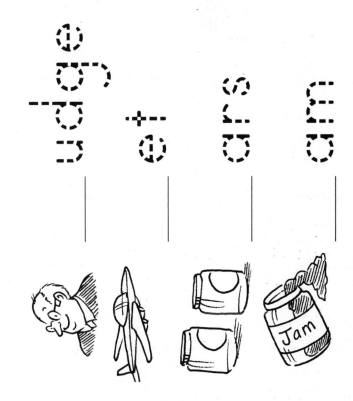

udge _____

jet _____

jars _____

jam _____

The judge
took a jet . . .

1

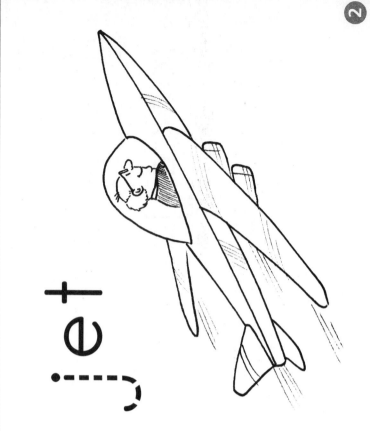

jet

2

jam

6

The judge
took a jet
to buy jars
of jam.

5

3

Ken
and his kitten
gave a key...

Ken

key

hen _____
kitten _____
key _____
king _____

4

Ken
and his kitten . . .

kitten

king

Ken
and his kitten
gave a key
to the king.

The lizard
on the ladder
likes to leap . . .

The Lizard

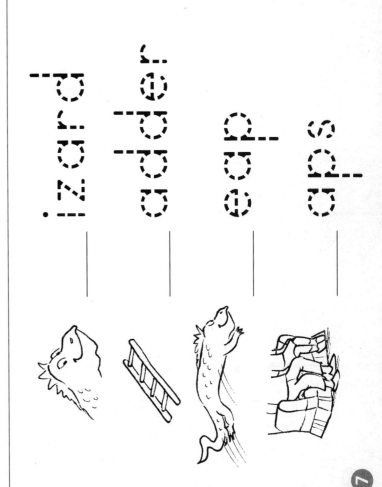

leap

lizard

ladder

leap

laps

1

The lizard
on the ladder...

2

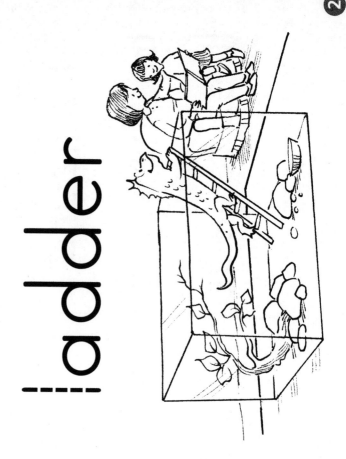

ladder

6

laps

5

The lizard
on the ladder
likes to leap
onto laps.

A man
in a movie
saw a monster . . .

A Man

26 Read & Write Mini-Books: Beginning Sounds From A to Z Scholastic Teaching Resources

monster

an _____

ovie _____

onster _____

oon _____

A man
in a movie . . .

movie

moon

A man
in a movie
saw a monster
on the moon.

Nate

Nate
had a net
and went north . . .

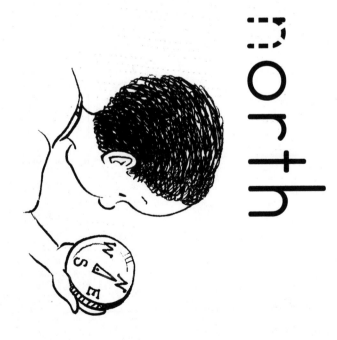

north

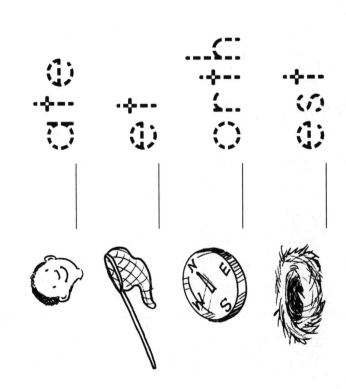

26 Read & Write Mini-Books: Beginning Sounds From A to Z   Scholastic Teaching Resources

Nate
had a net ...

net

nest

Nate
had a net
and went north
to a nest.

An ostrich
jumped over
an otter...

An Ostrich

otter

_strich

_ver

_tter

_cean

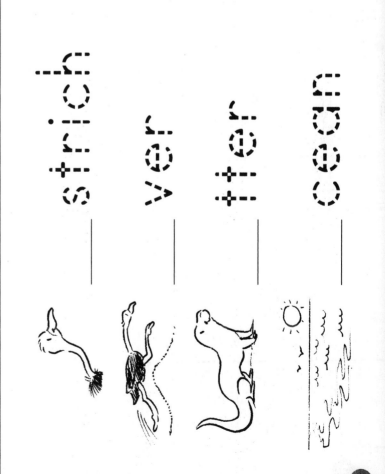

An ostrich
jumped over…

over

Ocean

An ostrich
jumped over
an otter
and into the ocean.

The penguin
took the path
to a party . . .

3

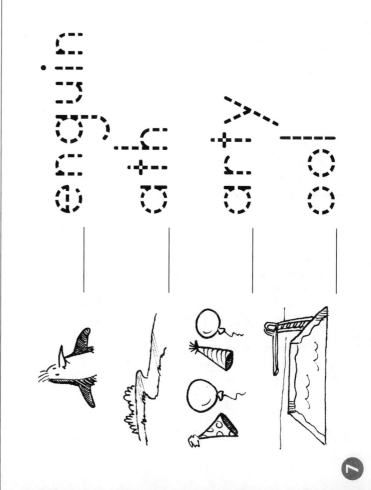

party

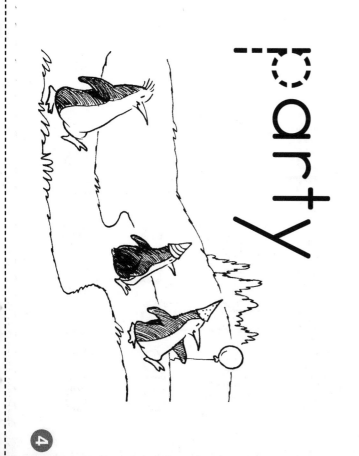

4

_enguin

_ath

_arty

_ool

7

The penguin
took the path . . .

path

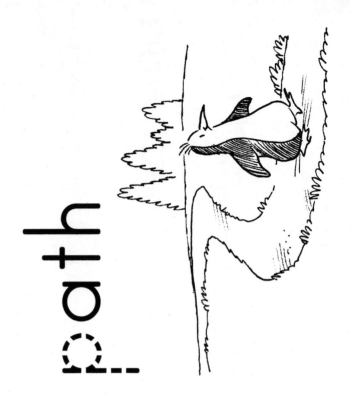

pool

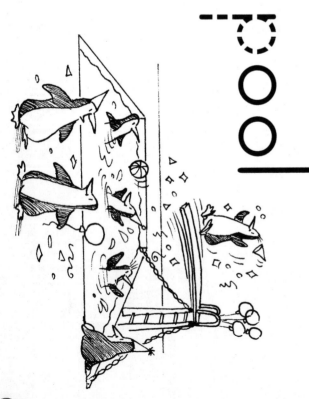

The penguin
took the path
to a party
at the pool.

The quail
paid a quarter
to buy a quilt . . .

The Quail

26 Read & Write Mini-Books: Beginning Sounds From A to Z   Scholastic Teaching Resources

quilt

quail

quarter

quilt

queen

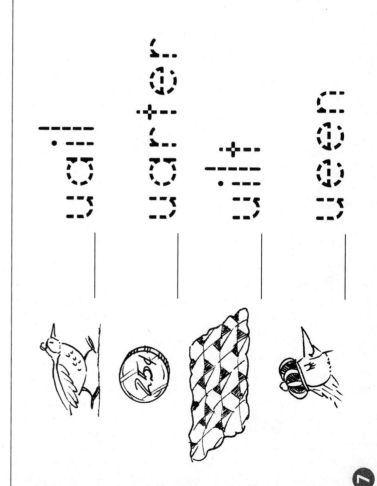

1

The quail
paid a quarter . . .

quarter

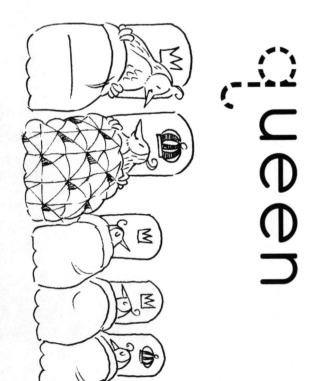

queen

6

The quail
paid a quarter
to buy a quilt
for the queen.

5

The rat
on the roof
likes to ride . . .

The Rat

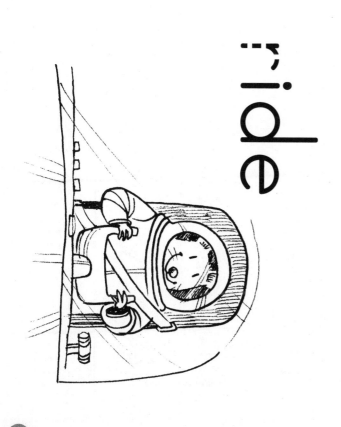

ride

_ _at

r_ _of

r_ _de

r_ _ocket

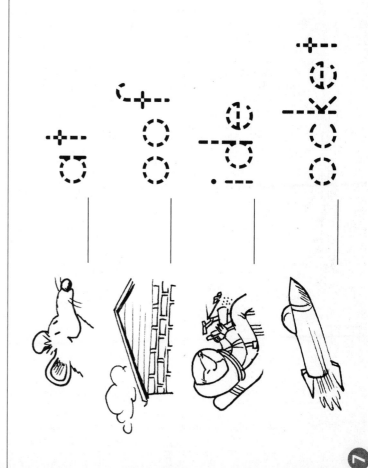

The rat
on the roof . . .

roof

rocket

The rat
on the roof
likes to ride
in a rocket.

A seal
in the sea
has a sack ...

A Seal

sack

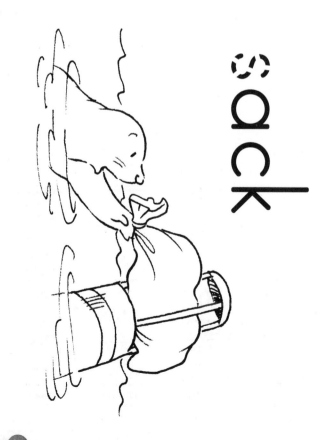

sea
sea
sack
sub

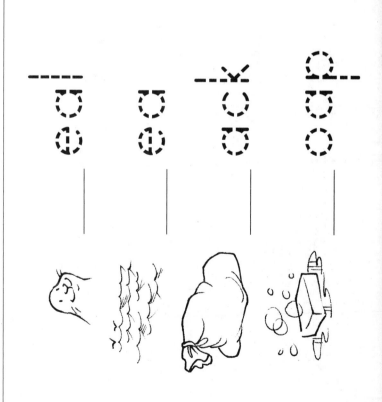

A seal
in the sea . . .

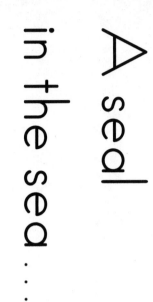

1

sea

2

soap

6

26 *Read & Write Mini-Books: Beginning Sounds From A to Z*   Scholastic Teaching Resources

A seal
in the sea
has a sack
with some soap.

5

Tina
had a ticket
to see tigers ...

Tina

tigers

ina

icket

igers

ee

Tina
had a ticket ...

ticket

toes

Tina
had a ticket
to see tigers
on their toes.

My uncle
got his umbrella
and we went up . . .

My Uncle

26 Read & Write Mini-Books: Beginning Sounds From A to Z   Scholastic Teaching Resources

up

__ ncle

__ mbrella

__ p

__ nicorn

1

My uncle got his umbrella....

2

umbrella

6

unicorn

5

My uncle got his umbrella, and we went up to see a unicorn.

Vic
drove the van
to the village . . .

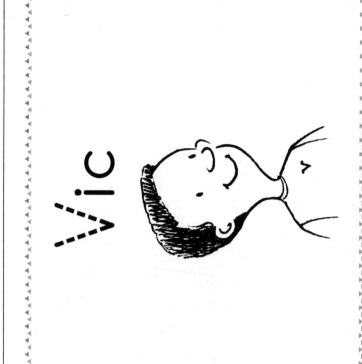

Vic

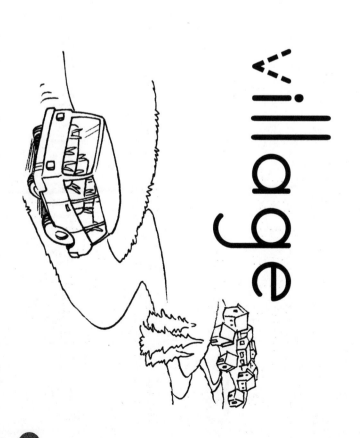

village

Vic

van

village

vegetables

Vic
drove the van . . .

van

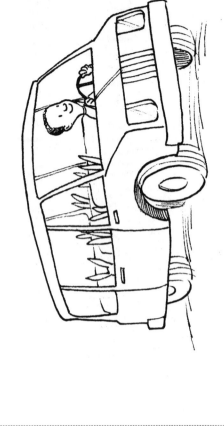

vegetables

Vic
drove the van
to the village
to buy vegetables.

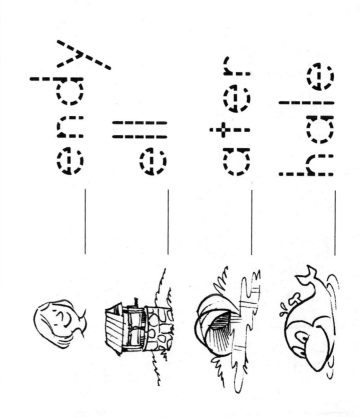

Wendy

Wendy
used the well
to get some water...

water

Wendy
well
water
and

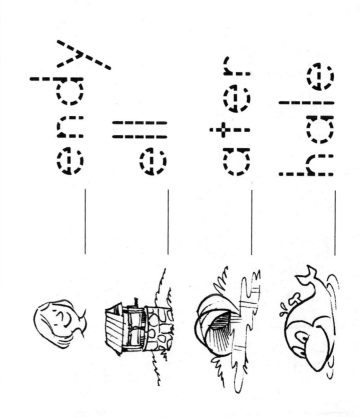

3

4

7

26 Read & Write Mini-Books: Beginning Sounds From A to Z Scholastic Teaching Resources

Wendy
used the well . . .

well

whale

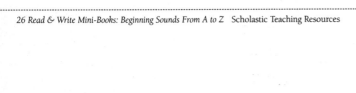

Wendy
used the well
to get some water
for her whale.

An ox
sent a box
to a fox . . . .

An Ox

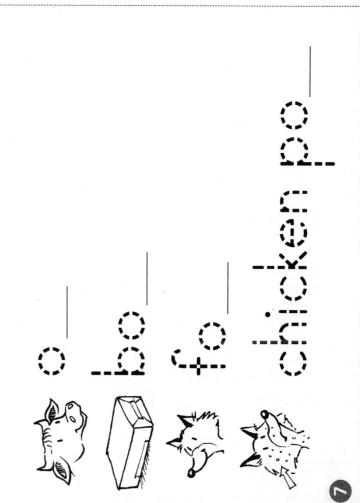

fox

To: Fox
From: Ox

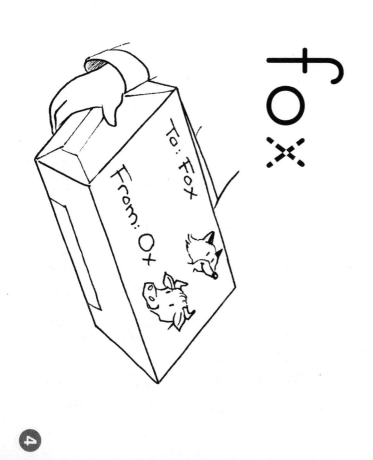

o___
b___
fo___
chicken po___

1

An ox
sent a box . . .

2

box

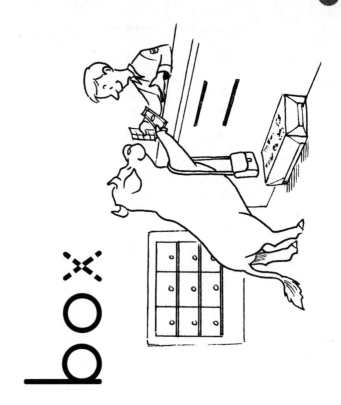

6

chicken
pox

5

An ox
sent a box
to a fox
with chicken pox.

Yan
has a yak
in her yard . . .

Yan

yard

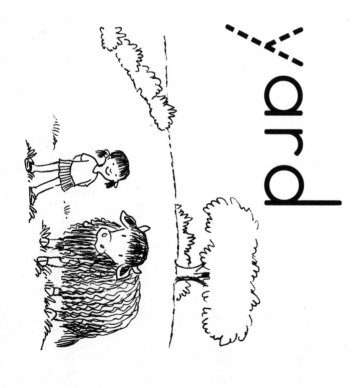

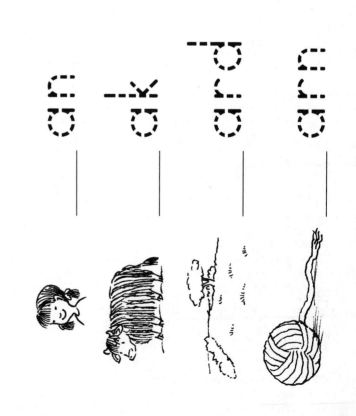

Yan

has a yak . . .

yak

yarn

Yan

has a yak
in her yard
that makes yarn.

Zack
had a zipper
that went zip . . .

Zack

26 Read & Write Mini-Books: Beginning Sounds From A to Z   Scholastic Teaching Resources

zip

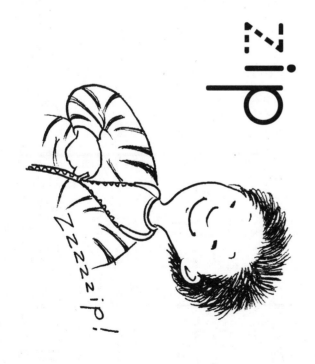

Zzzzzzip!

_ _ ack

_ ipper

_ ip

_ebra

zzzip!

Zack
had a zipper . . .

zipper

zebra

Zack
had a zipper
that went zip
when he was a zebra.